May 14, 1995

To Mother
on Mother's Day!
Enjoy ... with all my love

Warren.

Whistling Wings

The Beauty Of Ducks In Flight

Stephen Kirkpatrick

Whistling Wings
The Beauty Of Ducks In Flight

Published by

Thy Marvelous Works

P. O. BOX 31414
Jackson, MS 39286-1414

First Edition

Printed & bound by
Kingsport Press, Kingsport, TN

Color separations by
Kaminer & Welch, Jackson, MS

Graphic Artist
Sam Beibers

Library of Congress Catalog #89-50221

ISBN # O-9619353-3-2 (Trade)
ISBN # O-9619353-4-O (Deluxe)

To my sons, Sean and Ryan, may all of Creation forever enrich your lives.

WHISTLING WINGS has been a long time in the making. It would not have come into being without the help of many people, to whom I say "Thank You". I would particularly like to thank Mr. Kaneaster Hodges for his enthusiastic support and friendship. Also, I would like to thank Mr. Bill Walker and Mr. Bob Harris for the photographic opportunities they have afforded me in the past.

I would like to thank all the members of my family for their always "being there" when I needed them most. Their strength has kept the vision alive. A special thanks to my wife Marian who has given up much to see these pages come to life.

To you Lord Jesus I give all the glory. You have touched my ounce of talent with gallons of opportunity and blessing. No amount of human wisdom and effort could replace that. I love you.

Then God said, "Let the birds fly above the earth in the open expanse of the heavens." (Genesis 1:20)

PREFACE

*F*light has always been one of man's greatest fascinations. Ever since the beginning of time he has always wanted to "fly like a bird". Even now with all of our airplanes, rockets and advanced technology we still marvel at natural flight. We watch and yearn to feel the wind's lifting power, defeating gravity's pull. We sense the wonder of lift off, the joy of accelleration and the poetic fervor of descending for a landing.

The ability to capture these emotional moments and present them on the printed page is difficult. The use of photography does help. Photography is simply "to write with light". Taking shadows, highlights, form, color and all their combinations we begin to see why it is said that a picture is worth a thousand words. However, to transcend paper and ink and to form emotional paragraphs in the mind, more is needed. We must add to this our imagination…mere pictures and words are not enough…

CONTENTS

INTRODUCTION

I can't remember when it was that I first fell in love with ducks. It may have been when I was 7 years old on my first hunting trip. I had crawled up on some coots, thinking they were ducks, and felt as if I had out witted the smartest of the smart! Or maybe it was years later when I raised those pet mallards in my backyard in south Louisiana. I remember bringing a drake to show my mother while she was washing dishes. He got loose and raised quacking havoc, scaring my mother half to death. Chasing him all over the kitchen I finally caught him. I spent the rest of the evening cleaning up the "mess".

Whatever the case, I have always been intrigued by ducks. Like millions of others, ducks hold a unique place in my heart. They, of late, have definitely come into their own. Even though the duck stamp craze has gotten a bit out of hand and has somewhat worn out the subject, ducks still capture the hearts of men whenever they are seen. It's not only hunters that are excited at the sight of them but birders, naturalists, zoo patrons, just about anyone who frequents and savors natures blessings. I'm not sure just why they touch us like they do but they do.

Most people associate ducks with water. By describing an awkward scene or situation, they often are heard to say, "like a duck out of water". True enough, when they are walking on land they are a bit awkward, but when they take to the skies they are masters! The sights and sounds of their aerodynamic flight patterns are a touching spectacle in themselves.

If you have ever stood at lands end near an open marsh or wooded swamp you know the feelings. The cupped wings of a flight of mallards, the screaming cry of an exiting wood duck or the tearing rush of blue-winged teal all cause the human heart to pound. Peace floods your soul and you stand in awe. Humbly you look skyward knowing that you are close to the heartbeat of God. It is something that is hard to describe, it needs to be experienced.

The following pages are not that of an ID guide or a
biological survey of waterfowl. It's an aesthetic experience; a
simple viewing of the beauty of ducks in flight. A pleasurable
time of removing oneself from the rigors of the day to drift
out into nature. These pages could never replace the real
thing nor are they meant to. They should simply bring us to a
place of remembrance and help us momentarily fly with
those masters of the sky.

Each time I am out with the Lord's creations I feel His
warmth encompassing me. To some of us the chance to see
a flight of ducks in the sky is more satisfying than all television
has to offer and to hear the sound of beating wings is much
more important than a rally on Wall Street. So for now we
turn the pages slowly, absorbing all that enriches our spirit. Sitting entranced by the sight of our feathered friends we quiet-
ly listen. As we recall, through the calm, we can hear those
soothing sounds of *WHISTLING WINGS . . .*

I. *Solos*

$\mathcal{S}$olo simply means to be alone. This may be a choice or it may not be a choice but the fact remains that there is only one. A duck all alone is a somewhat unique occurance. Ducks are gregarious creatures and according to Webster this means: "sociable, a flock, fond of the company of others". Just why a duck would be alone is a study in itself.

A duck that is solo is a thing of beauty. A quick observation will reveal information about him. Quacking frantically often tells us a mate is lost or being looked for. Being alone may even be a choice, as in flying over others to get to a solitary setting. Sometimes a lone duck is a leader preparing for migration or ready to leave for another location. He may even be an outcast, sick or wounded.

Whatever the case, a solo duck causes us to focus on him. Photographs give us the ability to examine them with careful eyes. Muddy feet or a duckweed covered breast tell us where he has been. Feathers can tell us age. Body position can tell us his next move. These observations should not take away from their beauty but add to our knowledge, enhancing the total experience.

Solos, here they come, one at a time...

WOOD DUCK

Mississippi, Oct. 1988

*Coming in before sunrise I had to wait. He swam closer to me
as the morning progressed. Mornings first rays hit my back
and I pointed and shot. He decided to eat somewhere else!*

14

600mm, 1/1000 @ f4, K64

MALLARD

Mississippi, Mar. 1988

The calm surface is soon to be broken.
Coming in from behind me I almost didn't see him.

400mm, 1/1000 @ f3.5, K64

MALLARD

Arkansas, Jan. 1989

One ray of light strikes this lone drake, and separates him from the shaded background. I was concerned about exposure, it was dead on.

400mm, 1/1000 @ f3.5, K64

WOOD DUCK

Louisiana, Feb. 1988

Flying through trees is usually reserved for songbirds but it is the Wood Ducks specialty, fog and all.

400mm, 1/1000 @ f3.5, K64

RING-NECKED DUCK

Mississippi, Dec. 1985

*Looking for friends his attention was elsewhere. It must have been.
I was departing the swamp in clear view late one afternoon
when I swung around and got off this one shot!*

300mm, 1/000 @ f4.5, K64

BUFFLEHEAD

Mississippi, Jan. 1987

*The striking black and white markings of the Bufflehead make him a
photographic challenge. Here solo but not alone he follows the footsteps
of the earlier departing female.*

400mm, 1/1000 @ f4, K64

WOOD DUCK

Mississippi, Nov. 1988

Letting all of his friends know that he has arrived,
he is unaware that I am informed also.

400mm. 1/1000 @ f3.5, K64

WOOD DUCK

Mississippi, Jun. 1988

*It was a beautiful cool summer sunrise. As I surveyed the landscape
a single woody sailed in over the cattails. Mornings like this
will bring you back time and time again.*

400mm, 1/1000 @ f5.6, K64

RING-NECKED DUCK

Mississippi, Nov. 1985

For all practical purposes this guy has pinpointed his landing site.
With his head level and body twisted he reacts to and with wind currents.
Breaking down air speed he positions decent.

300mm, 1/1000 @ f4.5, K64

WIGEON

Mississippi, Dec. 1986

There was a shallow crossing between two low areas in a flooded field. The ducks were using it to cross back and forth as they fed. I was set up near the narrow crossing, this one didn't make it to the other side!

400mm, 1/1000 @ f4, K64

WOOD DUCK

Mississippi, Nov. 1988

A squealing answer to his searching cry brings a quick decision to land.
The "falling brick" decent is put into action.

400mm, 1/1000 @ f4, K64

MALLARD

Mississippi, Nov. 1988

Gear down, flaps back. Don't hit the Gadwall!
Two full wing beats and splash down.

400mm, 1/1000 @ f4, K64

BLUE-WINGED TEAL

Mississippi, Mar. 1987

*This photo has a special meaning to me. Not only do I remember
sneaking up on him to get the picture (which is nearly impossible to do),
but it was an instrumental part of getting this book actually "started"
after appearing on a magazine cover.
It sparked letters from an outside source that proved
to be a sign from above to keep going! Thank you, Mrs. Lynch.*

400mm, 1/1000 @ f4, K64

MALLARD

Mississippi, Dec. 1988

The cloudy sunset reveals a curled tail
that gives the identifying mark needed.

400mm, 1/1000 @ f11, K64

GADWALL

Louisiana, Dec. 1988

*He never saw me. After landing he sensed something was wrong
and his departure was definitely not "poetry in motion."*

400mm, 1/1000 @ f4, K64

MALLARD

Mississippi, Nov. 1987

*Soft light, soft colors and a soft landing make for a
calming portrait of the Susie.*

400mm, 1/500 @ f3.5, K64

GADWALL

Mississippi, Nov. 1987

He must have gotten full and left a duckweed covered swamp.
He may be coming here to rest, the others in front of me are.

400mm, 1/1000 @ f4, K64

RING-NECKED DUCK

Mississippi, Nov. 1984

Duck!! I nearly had to. He busted out right over my submerged body.

300mm, 1/1000 @ f4.5, K64

MALLARD

Mississippi, Dec. 1988

*Late afternoon light colors this lone drake in search of company,
he found it.*

400mm, 1/1000 @ f3.5, K64

MALLARD

Florida, May 1982

The rear view of a descending duck is not an easy shot to get.
It's interesting to note where the feet are placed when the duck
is in this position. This is the oldest photo in the book.

300mm, 1/250 @ f4.5, K64

II. _Duos_

_W_hen we think of a duo we often think of a pair, male and female. While this may often be true, it certainly is not the rule. Throughout the year immatures will team up, male with male and female with female. You will even see different species together from time to time. All of these appearing as friendships, comrads, or children at play. Sometimes looking for others, sometimes seeking solitude but drawn together for some reason.

We often see duos, especially pairs, within larger groups. They are easily spotted due to their close proximity and often similar flight patterns. A duck in such a case will often mirror anothers movements, creating interesting images for our eyes. Sometimes even distorting light, throwing shadows on the other. Whatever the case duos are interesting. Unlike solos, we are touched more by the interaction of elements than the elements themselves.

Duos, two's company...

MALLARDS

Louisiana, Nov. 1988

Headed who knows where, these two drakes are leaving.
The others are obviously considering doing the same.

400mm, 1/1000 @ f3.5, F50

GREEN-WINGED TEAL

Arkansas, Jan. 1989

Not an easy duck to get on film in any light much less heavy fog!

400mm, 1/1000 @ f3.5, K64

MALLARDS

Mississippi, Jan. 1987

Being only a day or two before the full moon, it rose early.
It was a perfect pass.

400mm, 1/1000 @ f5.6, K64

MALLARDS

Florida, Oct. 1984

*What a picture, mallards, moss and cypress. The broken light and
feathered iridescence gives us the "blue-head mallard"!*

300mm, 1/500 @ f4.5, K64

MALLARDS

Arkansas, Jan. 1989

Coming to a midday resting place,
this pair arrives and hits its classic breakdown position.

400mm, 1/1000 @ f4, K64

WOOD DUCKS

Mississippi, Oct. 1987

*These two immature male woodies are probably brothers. They will chum
around together until all of their colorful feathers have filled in. When the
females answer back they will part company.*

400mm, 1/1000 @ f4, K64

GADWALLS

Mississippi, Dec. 1988

This pair pass in poetic form, on their second pass they set down.

400mm, 1/1000 @ f4, K64

RING-NECKED DUCKS

Mississippi, Mar. 1987

*The Mississippi delta farm country provides a perfect
sanctuary for this pair of late migrants North.*

400mm, 1/1000 @ f3.5, K64

GADWALLS

Mississippi, Nov. 1985

Very late one afternoon several flights of gadwalls had come in so I waited. As I was about to leave due to darkness, these two came floating in. The wonderful sidelight does them well. I guess this was their "best" side.

300mm, 1/500 @ f4.5, K64

FULVOUS WHISTLING-DUCKS

Texas, Jun. 1983

I was searching for prairie wildflowers when I stumbled upon these two.
The 6 inches of water and hard ground they jumped out of
was certainly not like my Mississippi swamp!

300mm, 1/500 @ f4.5, K64

MALLARDS

Mississippi, Dec. 1985

I can still remember this one. It was late afternoon about "dark-thirty".
My arms tired from holding the big 400mm and company
for nearly 4 hours! Earlier I had broken ice for half a mile to get there.
I watched several thousand ducks come in that afternoon. These two
made a late pass and the "Wary Lady" saw me, he obviously didn't.
Shortly they joined the thunderous gathering that was,
as I described, "over yonder".

400mm, 1/1000 @ f3.5, K64

BLACK DUCKS

Quebec, Canada, Aug. 1988

*Scouting late one afternoon I spotted a deer and my sons and I
drifted into the rocky cove. Noticing some movement down in the reeds
I focused my camera and saw the rare pair.
As we closed in on them they came exploding out. Got 'em!*

400mm, 1/1000 @ f3.5, K64

PINTAILS

Mississippi, Dec. 1985

Beneath incoming storm clouds these two pintails are set off
by the warming late afternoon sunlight.

300mm, 1/1000 @ f4.5, K64

WOOD DUCKS

Mississippi, Dec. 1988

Yes, she is in flight! Well, a form of it anyway. Notice the initial lift of the wings off of her back before they come crashing down into the water.

400mm, 1/1000 @ f4, K64

REDHEADS

Louisiana, Nov. 1988

*An uncommon visitor to this area. These two make one pass
and that's it. Just a short stop on their way to the coastal marshes.*

400mm, 1/1000 @ f4, K64

MALLARDS

Mississippi, Jan. 1984

What can I say, this was probably the most difficult shot to accomplish
in the entire book. Taken about 20 minutes after sunset,
the 25 degree weather gave the sky its magic!
They hit a near perfect silhouette as they come "Settlin' In."

300mm, 1/250 @ f4.5, K64

III. *Trios*

Three's a crowd, as in who's this guy honey? Or maybe three's company, as in misery loves company. Or maybe three's family, as in here comes junior! No matter how you say it "three" seems to mean odd man out. Yet in mathematics and creation three is the very definition of balance and harmony. The mind even perceives things in threes and is moved by it. The law of thirds, in design, is a perfect example where the sections of thirds cross as power points.

Three ducks in flight can touch us in a pleasing way by their arrangement or cause us to react by their seemingly "disarrangement". Three ducks in flight are far less common than you think. In working on this book I noticed out of the thousands of slides I sorted through to choose these shots, trios were the least common of any group. An interesting observation I thought.

Trio, an odd number yet it is the very foundation of our existance. A number of the Devine, stability, complement. Three, natures wonder.

Trios, points of interest...

MALLARDS

Mississippi, Jan. 1988

I'm glad I got a picture of this "double V" because within 15 minutes of this shot the bottom fell out of the clouds. I was over a mile from my jeep and it was all I could do to keep my camera dry.

400mm, 1/500 @ f3.5, K64

RING-NECKED DUCKS

Mississippi, Nov. 1984

*Coming in at water level with my head and camera the only things
above the surface, I waited for them to spook, they did.*

300mm, 1/1000 @ f5.6, K64

WOOD DUCKS

Mississippi, Nov. 1987

Joe Mac had taken me to his "fantastic(?)" wood duck hole. While in the blind (7 hours) we saw a raccoon, a green-backed heron and thought (?) we heard a duck land behind us. Got this one on our way out!

400mm, 1/1000 @ f4, K64

GREEN-WINGED TEAL

Mississippi, Dec. 1986

The lead drake shows that silvery underside that often appears as a blur
when these speedy fliers tear by!

400mm, 1/1000 @ f4, K64

RING-NECKED DUCKS

Arkansas, Feb. 1989

*A thunderstorm forms an enhancing backdrop for these Ringnecks
in diffused light. Their golden eyes are the only color seen.*

400mm, 1/1000 @ f3.5, K64

MALLARDS

Mississippi, Dec. 1985

*It's hard to get the sun to shine underneath a duck but
when it does it makes a wonderful picture!*

300mm, 1/1000 @ f4.5, K64

GADWALL & SHOVELERS

Mississippi, Mar. 1987

*This was taken while working an area in a camouflaged innertube.
I like it! As they say here in Mississippi "a blind hog finds an acorn
every now and then".*

400mm, 1/1000 @ f5.6, K64

SHOVELERS

Mississippi, Feb. 1986

What a perfect formation. Even their wing tips are split the same.
Doubt I'll ever see this again, especially with the lady leading!

400mm, 1/1000 @ f5.6, K64

MALLARDS

Mississippi, Dec. 1985

Stacked and falling in! These three have found what they were looking for. Maybe you can hear the others calling them down.

300mm, 1/1000 @ f4, K64

GADWALLS

Mississippi, Nov. 1988

I just like this picture. Don't really know why. Must be the hues and composition. The split sky in the background is an approaching storm.

400mm, 1/1000 @ f5.6, K64

WIGEON

Mississippi, Nov. 1987

*The early morning hues give a beautiful feel to this
decending threesome.*

400mm, 1/500 @ f3.5, K64

BLUE-WINGED TEAL

Mississippi, Aug. 1984

These early migrants still don't have their winter plumage.
A short stop here and it's on to Central America.

300mm, 1/1000 @ f4.5, K64

MALLARDS

Mississippi, Nov. 1985

*This classic threesome appears motionless as their powerful wings resist
gravity's pull. Within seconds they will splash down
into the stump filled swamp.*

300mm, 1/1000 @ f4.5, K64

WOOD DUCKS

Mississippi, Nov. 1988

*Headed across the sun, these three woodies make a stunning site
for my tired eyes. Many of my sunset shots are the last photos taken
after a very long day in the field.*

400mm, 1/1000 @ f11, K64

IV. *Squadrons*

*W*hen we think of a squad we think of a team. It's large enough to get the job done yet small enough for its members to be recognized as individuals. As they intermingle the elements work together as a unit. These organized groups seem as though they have gotten together for a purpose, unlike solos, duos and trios which seem to set themselves apart.

A portrait of social life can be seen while watching these groups. In flight they often take on formations reminding us of Air Force flight patterns. Wings cutting paths as they play off the air currents of each other. Sometimes they quickly swerve and bump, intentional and accidental! We observe their actions and habits and wonder why they are together. Some are leaders, some are lookouts and some simply tag along. They are often seen quacking, even biting at each other. Are they all from the same family? Do they all have the same destination? They could be outcasts, forced together for some reason. We don't always know but they sure are touching sights together.

The beauty of a squadron touches more than the eye. Their bond, working for the common good, sparks something deep in our soul. Each individual member functioning in its God given place bringing together both design and function. Working with the elements they leave an impression on our mind. Inspiring!

Squadrons, seeing the whole by its parts...

BLACK DUCKS

Mississippi, Dec. 1985

I get excited when I see Blacks. I don't see them much anymore,
much less get pictures.

400mm, 1/1000 @ f4, K64

BLUE-WINGED TEAL

Arkansas, May 1988

These migrants were somewhat late getting to their northern breeding grounds this being mid-May! The wooded background and late afternoon light make for a favorite photo.

400mm, 1/1000 @ f3.5, K64

SHOVELERS

Mississippi, Dec. 1983

I still remember sitting in cattails waiting for this one. Normally gone by mid-morning, I decided to stay. The high, side light is the right touch, but wing positions and "spoonbills" make it for me!

300mm, 1/1000 @ f5.6, K64

GADWALLS

Arkansas, Feb. 1989

Highlighted bellies and underwings in the light morning mist.
Words are insufficent...

400mm, 1/1000 @ f3.5, K64

GADWALLS

Mississippi, Nov. 1988

"Gabbing and grabbing", gadwalls do this often seemingly for no reason.
The approaching storm made a nice backdrop for these children at play.

400mm, 1/1000 @ f4, K64

PINTAILS

Arkansas, Jan. 1989

They circled five different times before choosing their landing spot.
I guess the heavy fog made them a little more careful than usual.
I love this light.

400mm, 1/1000 @ f3.5, K64

RING-NECKED DUCKS

Mississippi, Nov. 1985

Five and five. Composition and light give this shot
all the needed ingredients.

300mm, 1/1000 @ f4.5, K64

GADWALLS

Louisiana, Mar. 1989

This shot was not even an honest try. I had completed a year long job and walked down to the waters edge behind the lodge to reminisce and relax. I had carried my camera along and took a few shots of some ducks out on the lake at sunset. What can I say!

400mm, 1/2000 @ f8, K64

GADWALLS

Arkansas, Jan. 1989

*Ridin' the fog. This flock seems to stay right above the ground fog
while in search of a place to set down.*

400mm, 1/2000 @ f3.5, K64

MALLARDS

Louisiana, Dec. 1988

Uncomfortable and belly down in 2 inches of water I waited.
Several mallards landed just off from the shore. As I squirmed
trying to get into position for a shot they jumped and I fired.
Quite honestly I was surprised at the results.

400mm, 1/1000 @ f4, K64

WIGEON & GADWALLS

Louisiana, Dec. 1988

*The sun had not come over the horizon yet but this group was
high enough to catch the very first rays of the day.
This is what I describe as "perfect light".*

400mm, 1/1000 @ f3.5, K64

GADWALLS

Louisiana, Jan. 1989

The ducks were resting on the open water during the day and feeding in the bean fields at night. Many more were yet to come by.

400mm, 1/1000 @ f5.6, K64

MALLARDS

Mississippi, Dec. 1985

*Cupped wings, patterned clouds and strong composition
give this shot strength to make the final edit!*

300mm, 1/1000 @ f4.5, K64

WIGEON

Mississippi, Dec. 1986

"Whiffling: to shift or veer about; vacillate." That is exactly what you see here. Ducks often do this to break down air speed and drop quickly. What happens is the "Bernoulli" affect is broken when the airfoil (lift) is removed as the birds flip their wings, sometimes nearly upside down.

400mm, 1/1000 @ f3.5, K64

PINTAILS

Mississippi, Nov. 1985

*The first picture with my new lens was one that gave me the impression
that I was going to like it!*

400mm, 1/1000 @ f4, K64

RING-NECKED DUCKS

Mississippi, Nov. 1985

A flight of ringnecks is an exciting site, but they sound even better!
They "tear" through the atmosphere with a loud and distinctive sound.
It thrills the soul and rushes the blood.

300mm, 1/1000 @ f4.5, K64

WOOD DUCKS

Mississippi, Nov. 1988

Getting this one was no easy chore.
Finally a shot of the ones that "didn't get away".

400mm, 1/1000 @ f5.6, K64

WOOD DUCKS

Mississippi, Nov. 1988

*I remember this shot like it was yesterday. I had just started my 45
minute walk out of the swamp when I saw them coming out of the
blazing red sunset. I got off a few shots before they nearly hit me!
I looked down...1/500...too slow I thought.
This shot was truely a gift from above. Thank you Lord.*

400mm, 1/500 @ f3.5, K64

v. *Wings*

*W*e as humans have to admit we all have a hang up with numbers. We forever want more, more, more! The revealing question is more of what and what for. In this case more ducks. When I think of hundreds or thousands of wings I must admit I don't readily think of whistling as the word to describe them. If you have ever heard a large flock of ducks take off the sound is closer to that of a freight train than a whistle! But when those same wings are cupped and descending for a landing the sound ministers like sweet music to the ears. Now that's my kind of music!

For those of us who love ducks the sight of large numbers of them stirs the soul. It's not only the large number of ducks but the solos, duos, trios and squadrons within that interest us. Along with this are shades and hues of colors, shadows, spaces and shapes. All these make up the total experience.

A sigh is released, a mood is changed and memories are stirred to a day gone by. These sights will not soon vacate our memory. For within the whole we see the parts. Wings mixed with wings, and within we feel at home. Whistling wings, something comfortable we slip into once in a while.

Wings, seeing a symphony…

MALLARDS

Mississippi, Jan. 1988

*Clouds yielded bad light, fog hindered focus and the dark background
made me question even trying. It was my "why not" attitude
that captured the pleasing image.*

400mm, 1/250 @ f3.5, K64

GREEN-WINGED TEAL

Mississippi, Jan. 1987

Flights of teal whiz by as their nervous and gregarious personalities show forth.

400mm, 1/1000 @ f5.6, K64

GADWALLS

Louisiana, Dec. 1988

*Flying into wooded cover before sunrise, the sight of them dodging
the branches was worth the wait.*

400mm, 1/1000 @ f3.5, K64

RING-NECKED DUCKS

Mississippi, Nov. 1985

The definitive portrait of a flight of ringnecks.

300mm, 1/1000 @ f4.5, K64

WOOD DUCKS, GADWALLS & MALLARDS

Mississippi, Nov. 1988

*Moving on to their nightime feeding grounds, these noisy migrants
silhouette against a wonderfully clear sunset.*

400mm, 1/1000 @ f4, K64

MALLARDS

Mississippi, Jan. 1988

*I had returned from a mornings outing and was eating a sandwich.
Someone came in the lodge and said I should come see the thousands
of mallards working this field. I looked outside and saw the miserable
conditions and said "this is a day for ducks". It was!*

400mm, 1/500 @ f3.5, K64

BLUE-WINGED TEAL

Mississippi, Sep. 1985

*Foggy morning silhouettes over delta farm country. They made at least a
dozen passes before settling in.*

300mm, 1/1000 @ f4.5, K64

MALLARDS

Louisiana, Jan. 1989

*The American Sportsman with Curt Gowdy and company had filmed
here two days earlier. That is not what I remember about this place
though. It's not even the 28 degree, windy and overcast day I remember.
What I remember is the stump hole I fell in on my way to the blind,
the two shivering hours attempting to get a picture and the root
I hooked my toe on flipping me headlong into the muddy bottom
on my way out! Isn't this fun...*

400mm, 1/1000 @ f3.5, K64

GREEN-WINGED TEAL

Arkansas, Jan. 1989

The loosely structured flight of the Teal is easily identified. Here they choose a late morning rest area and soon "fall" out of the sky.

400mm, 1/2000 @ f3.5, K64

MALLARDS

Mississippi, Dec. 1987

These mallards make their way south as a Red-tailed Hawk looks on.

400mm, 1/1000 @ f4, K64

CANVASBACKS

Mississippi, Dec. 1986

We don't see a lot of canvasbacks here in Mississippi.
These were moving through in "V" formation late one afternoon.

400mm, 1/500 @ f3.5, K64

WOOD DUCKS

Mississippi, Nov. 1988

Through the cattails and out of the sun.
Late afternoon woodies head to the open marsh for the night.

400mm, 1/2000 @ f8, K64

MALLARDS

Mississippi, Dec. 1985

Hundreds were circling, no kidding! The fields were frozen but that didn't stop them. For a couple of hours they just kept coming, one group right after another...as seen here.

400mm, 1/1000 @ f4, K64

MALLARDS

Mississippi, Dec. 1986

*Thousands were out there. Here the big lens grabs only a section of
them as they lift off. An intrigueing mist falls from their feet and wings.
I wish you could have heard it, the noise was deafening!*

400mm, 1/1000 @ f4, K64

PINTAILS

South Carolina, Feb. 1987

A terrible Atlantic storm hit the coast bringing with it lots of rain and high winds. I know, I was in it! I was happy to get this shot of pintails working their way up the coast.

400mm, 1/1000 @ f5.6, K200

SCAUP

South Carolina, Feb. 1987

This picture was taken from the same spot the following morning of the previous photo. The storm had obviously run its course and this beautiful sunrise served as a wonderful backdrop for another group of ducks moving up the coast.

400mm, 1/1000 @ f5.6, K64

PINTAILS & GADWALLS

Mississippi, Jan. 1987

*Late evening sun bounces off of the clouds as
the ducks within head for evening shelter.*

400mm, 1/1000 @ f5.6, K64

MALLARDS & PINTAILS

Mississippi, Dec. 1986

*After 2 1/2 days of rain I packed my bags. As I was leaving I looked
north and saw blue sky as a front was pushing its way in quickly.
Immediatly I headed out. I knew the birds were working a certain area
so I put a 75 degree angle of sunlight on it and waited.
I counted about 700 come in, then I got them up. What, no hens?*

400mm, 1/1000 @ f4, K64

PHOTO FACTS

The 97 photographs in *WHISTLING WINGS* were not selected without some amount of agony. From the original edit of my files I ended up with 1100 slides of ducks in flight. After several sessions of throwing out slides that were not in keeping with the purpose of the book, I got it down to 223 slides. From then on it was a slow grueling process of removing one at a time.

Many of the slides that were culled out were close to my heart and brought back memorable experiences. That's where it got hard, those personal favorites! I feel I managed to keep my emotions out of the way long enough to accomplish the purpose of this book.

As you can imagine none of these shots were easily gotten. Many a roll of film, a lot of sweat and "muucho" miles of marsh and swamp were walked to get them. I remember one morning when I broke ice around a tree in order to sit down and hide in the water. I shoved my feet down into the mud and pulled some cover around me and began my wait for the ducks. They soon came by the hundreds. I shot 7 rolls of 36 exposure film. I was so cold after a couple of hours that I could not hold the camera steady even on a support. I decided to leave and I couldn't, I was becoming part of the frozen lake! Not one of those photos made the book!

For what it's worth I have provided some statistics below. You may notice that many shots were hand held and ask why. The main reason is I work a lot of Mississippi swamps and there is no bottom to speak of. This makes any form of support useless. Also the freedom that hand holding affords is a plus in the awkward situations I work in, especially with fast flying ducks. I have also developed a shoulder mount but haven't perfected it to my liking yet. It did produce 1 picture for the book though (page 30).

I use a "freestyle" approach to photography. I work mostly from natural cover found on the spot. This gives me the ability to set up where the birds are working. With this approach, I am also wet more often than dry and cold more often than warm!

My objective in photographing ducks in flight was to record on film images that had more to them than just "sharp focus". This alone was difficult. But by adding angled light, differing weather conditions and composition I hoped to bring the photos alive. I feel the enclosed images came close to what I ideally wanted.

CAMERAS

Nikon FE & F3

LENSES

Nikkor 300mm f4.5
Nikkor 400mm f3.5
Nikkor 600mm f4

TRIPODS

Leitz Tiltall
Slik U-212

FILM

Kodachrome 64
Kodachrome 200
Fujichrome 50

STATISTICS (of 97 total photos)

15 Species:

Mallard (32)
Gadwall (17)
Wood Duck (12)
Ringneck (9)
Pintail (5)
B. W. Teal (4)
G. W. Teal (4)
Wigeon (4)
Shoveler (3)
Black Duck (2)
Redhead (1)
Canvasback (1)
Fulvous Whistling-Duck (1)
Scaup (1)
Bufflehead (1)

7 Areas:

Mississippi (70)
Arkansas (11)
Louisiana (10)
Florida (2)
S. Carolina (2)
Texas (1)
Quebec (1)

5 Support Methods Used:

Monopod (37)
Hand Held (33)
Tripod (21)
Innertube (3)
Tree (2)
Shoulder Mount (1)

Photo Dates:

Oldest Photo – May 1982 (page 33)
Most Recent – March 1989 (page 77)

By Year	By Month	
1982 (1)	Jan (17)	Jul (0)
1983 (3)	Feb (7)	Aug (2)
1984 (5)	Mar (5)	Sep (1)
1985 (20)	Apr (1)	Oct (6)
1986 (8)	May (2)	Nov (26)
1987 (15)	Jun (2)	Dec (28)
1988 (32)		
1989 (13)		

ABOUT THE AUTHOR

Born Sept. 6, 1954, in Dover, Delaware Stephen Kirkpatrick soon moved with his Air Force family to Alaska. It was there in the Alaskan wilderness that his love for the outdoors began. But it wasn't until years later, when they finally settled in Southern Louisiana, that his love of the swamp took root. The abundance and diversity of wildlife should be reason enough to love photographing swamps "however" he says, "it's the moods and settings of all the contrasting elements that make the place a pleasure to work in."

Since becoming a full time professional he has found that photographing nature is a pleasure but making a living at it is another story indeed. "It takes a miracle for some shots to get before the camera much less on film or the printed page." It's not a glamorous job either. Bugs and spiders in your ears, mouth and down your neck not to mention the snakes and alligators. It's enough to deter even the most dedicated.

Kirkpatrick became a Christian and received his first camera in the same week in May of 1981. "It was no coincidence." Ever since then he has continued to grow in the Lord and learn the business and the art of photography. His art background from L.S.U. has served to be a great help in many aspects of photography and publishing.

His first publication, a book titled "FIRST IMPRESSIONS", is now sold out. He is now developing a line of limited edition lithographs, all signed and numbered and a series of "beauty" books the first of which is *WHISTLING WINGS*. He produces the state nature calendar "MISSISSIPPI MAGIC", works freelance jobs, produces multi-media slide shows and works special assignments. So far it seems to be working. Kirkpatrick has had nearly 400 published photos and has appeared in over 50 publications. He is Photography Editor for "THE CHRISTIAN OUT-DOORSMAN" magazine and a Nikon Professional Services member.

In the past couple of years he has had nearly 200 speaking engagements showing his very moving multi-media slide show "IMAGES OF GLORY". President Carter and some of his White House staff said they wanted to "take it home" after viewing it. But even with all this going on, Kirkpatrick has but one job before him, and that is, "to do the will of Him who called me". Their company name is a constant reminder that it is the Lord, not him, who creates the beautiful photographs. "I will praise Thee O Lord with my whole heart, I will show forth all "THY MARVELOUS WORKS." (Psalm 9:1).

Mr. Kirkpatrick now lives in Jackson, MS with his wife Marian and their two sons Sean (5) and Ryan (3).